Heretical Christianities

Exploring the Ebionites, Marcionites, and the Lost Doctrines That Shocked Orthodoxy

A Modern Translation

Adapted for the Contemporary Reader

Various Early Christian Sources

Translated by Tim Zengerink

© **Copyright 2025**
All rights reserved.

It is not legal to reproduce, duplicate, or transmit any part of this document in either electronic means or in printed format. Recording of this publication is strictly prohibited and any storage of this document is not allowed unless with written permission from the publisher except for the use of brief quotations in a book review.

This book contains works of fiction. Any resemblance to persons living or dead, or places, events, or locations is purely coincidental.

Table of Contents

Preface - Message to the Reader 1

Introduction 5

Gospel of the Ebionites & Fragments of Jewish-
    Christian Sects 10

    Fragment One 10
    Fragment Two 11
    Fragment Three 11
    Fragment Four 12
    Fragment Five 12
    Fragment Six 13
    Fragment Seven 13

Epistle of the Apostles & Patristic Excerpts 14

    Introduction 14
    Epistle of the Apostles 21

Thank You for Reading 48

Preface - Message to the Reader

What If You Could Help Rebuild the Greatest Library in Human History?

Thousands of years ago, the Library of Alexandria stood as the crown jewel of human achievement — a sanctuary where the collected wisdom of every known civilization was gathered, preserved, and shared freely.

And then, it was lost.

Through fire, conquest, and the slow erosion of time, humanity lost not just books — but ideas, dreams, discoveries, and stories that could have changed the world forever.

Today, the Library of Alexandria lives again — and you are invited to be a part of its restoration.

Our mission is simple yet profound:

To rebuild the greatest library the world has ever known, and to translate all timeless works into every language and dialect, so that no seeker of knowledge is ever left behind again.

By joining our movement to rebuild the modern Library of Alexandria, you become part of an unprecedented mission:

- **Unlimited Access to the Greatest Audiobooks & eBooks Ever Written:**

  Instantly explore thousands of legendary works—Plato, Shakespeare, Jane Austen, Leo Tolstoy, and countless more. All instantly available to read or listen, placing a complete literary universe at your fingertips.

- **Beautiful Paperback & Deluxe Editions at Printing Cost**

  Own any title as an elegant paperback, deluxe hardcover, or stunning collectible boxset—offered to you at true printing cost, delivered straight to your door. Build your personal Library of Alexandria, crafted for beauty, built for durability, and worthy of proud display.

- **Fresh Translations for Modern Readers—in Every Language & Dialect**

  Enjoy timeless masterpieces reimagined in clear, contemporary language—no more outdated phrases or obscure references. Alongside the original versions, we're tirelessly translating these classics into every language and dialect imaginable, ensuring accessibility and understanding across cultures and generations.

- **Join a Global Renaissance of Literature & Knowledge**

  You directly support expanding our library, publishing deluxe editions at true cost, translating works into all global languages, and bringing humanity's greatest stories to people everywhere. By joining today, you're not just preserving a legacy of masterpieces; you set in motion a powerful wave of literary accessibility.

Become a Torchbearer of Knowledge.

Join us for free now at **LibraryofAlexandria.com**

Together, we will ensure that the light of human wisdom never fades again.

With gratitude and a shared love of knowledge,
The Modern Library of Alexandria Team

Visit:

www.libraryofalexandria.com

Or scan the code below:

Introduction

Exploring the Ebionites, Marcionites, and the Lost Doctrines That Shocked Orthodoxy

In the shadow of what became mainstream Christianity lies a rich, tangled, and often misunderstood web of alternative Christian movements—voices once dismissed as heretical, but which were instrumental in shaping the boundaries of the faith we know today. These movements include the Jewish-Christian Ebionites, the dualist and rigorously grace-centered Marcionites, and the prophetic fervor of the Montanists. Each arose in the tumultuous centuries following the life of Jesus, during a period when Christian identity was anything but fixed. Together, they constitute what we now call the "heretical" Christianities—forgotten expressions of faith that dared to challenge, expand, or radically reinterpret the meaning of Christ and the Gospel.

A Spectrum of Forgotten Faiths

To understand the so-called heretical Christianities, one must first understand the fluid nature of early Christianity itself. In the first few centuries after Jesus' death, there was no single, unified doctrine or canon. Instead, there was a wide range of Christian expressions that were informed by regional, cultural, and theological differences. While the proto-orthodox movement—largely represented by figures such as Irenaeus, Tertullian, and Athanasius—would eventually shape the doctrine of the Church and the content of the New Testament, this was by no means inevitable or uncontested.

The Ebionites were Jewish-Christians who believed Jesus was the Messiah but rejected his divinity. They kept the Mosaic Law, honored the Torah, and viewed Paul as a deceiver who led the Gentiles astray. Their gospel—reconstructed from citations by Church Fathers—portrayed a deeply Torah-centered Jesus who was adopted as God's son at baptism. Their views were not fringe in the earliest years. In fact, their form of Christianity likely predated gentile Christianity, reflecting a version of the faith that was close to the Jerusalem Church led by James, the brother of Jesus.

Marcion, by contrast, took a radical approach: he completely rejected the Old Testament and its God, whom he saw as a lower, flawed deity distinct from the supreme God of Jesus Christ. To Marcion, Jesus revealed a gospel of pure grace, unconnected from the law, judgment, or wrath of the Hebrew Scriptures. His canon—consisting of a heavily edited Gospel of Luke and ten Pauline epistles—was the first known attempt at creating a formal Christian scripture. Marcion's theology forced the Church to clarify what it believed about the continuity between the Old and New Testaments. Ironically, it was his "heresy" that catalyzed the formation of the New Testament canon.

Then there were the Montanists, who emphasized ecstatic prophecy, the imminent return of Christ, and a highly ascetic lifestyle. Led by Montanus and female prophets such as Priscilla and Maximilla, the Montanist movement claimed that the Paraclete—the Spirit promised by Jesus—was speaking new revelations through them. Their ecstatic utterances and dramatic claims shook the early Church and posed a direct challenge to the authority of bishops and councils. Montanism was not rejected because it lacked passion or piety, but because it undermined the emerging ecclesiastical hierarchy.

The Winners Write the Canon

History, as always, is written by the victors. The Church Fathers who labeled these groups heretical did not do so from a neutral position. The Ebionites were condemned for "Judaizing" the faith; Marcion was excommunicated and denounced for mutilating scripture; the Montanists were vilified for their chaotic prophecies and spiritual elitism. Yet in their critiques, the Fathers preserved fragments of these groups' teachings—often quoting them at length in order to refute them. Ironically, these hostile citations are now among the only sources we have for reconstructing these marginalized voices.

What becomes clear when reading these texts and fragments is that the boundaries of Christianity were not clearly drawn in the early centuries. The doctrines we now accept as fundamental—Christ's divinity, the authority of the New Testament, the role of bishops— were fiercely debated. Heresy was not so much about error as it was about power, identity, and control.

The Gospel of the Ebionites, for example, omitted the virgin birth and emphasized Jesus' human nature and adherence to Jewish law. Marcion's canon elevated grace above all else and stripped away any hint of divine vengeance or tribal favoritism. The Montanists demanded holiness, ecstatic experience, and direct communion with God through prophecy—often placing themselves above bishops and scribes.

Despite their differences, these groups had something in common: each saw itself as the true heir to Jesus' message. They were not simply rebels or agitators; they were earnest believers, striving to live out the gospel as they understood it. They read the same scriptures (or versions of them), followed the same Christ, and often suffered the same persecutions. Yet their interpretations diverged so dramatically that they were ultimately excluded from the "Great Church."

By examining their texts today, we do not need to adopt their doctrines to appreciate their value. Rather, we can learn from their challenges, their questions, and their bold attempts to understand Jesus in their time and context. Their inclusion in this collection is not a celebration of division, but an acknowledgment that early Christianity was far more diverse—and far more fascinating—than later orthodoxy would admit.

This volume brings together the Gospel of the Ebionites, reconstructions of Marcion's canon, the prophetic oracles of the Montanists, and reflections from the Epistle of the Apostles and early patristic sources that help contextualize these movements. These writings are not just relics of the past; they are reminders that theology is always forged in struggle, and that even "heretics" helped define the faith they were accused of abandoning.

Let us now turn to the texts themselves and hear the voices that once challenged the shape of Christian tradition—voices that echo with courage, conviction, and an unrelenting pursuit of divine truth.

Gospel of the Ebionites & Fragments of Jewish-Christian Sects

The Ebionites were some of the earliest followers of Jesus, closely connected to the first Jewish-Christians known as the Nazarenes. Their name comes from the Hebrew word ebyonim, meaning "the poor," because they chose to live in poverty.

According to early Church leaders, this Lost Gospel is believed to have been written in the First or Second Century. Parts of it have been found in seven fragments, quoted in the writings of Epiphanius. The text suggests that neither John nor Jesus ate meat, and that Jesus did not support animal sacrifice.

Below is the English translation of the fragments from the Lost Gospel of the Ebionites.

Fragment One

During the time of Herod, the ruler of Judea, and while Caiaphas was the chief priest, John appeared at the Jordan River, baptizing people as a sign of their commitment to change their ways.

He was believed to be a descendant of Aaron and was the son of Elizabeth and Zacharias, who was a priest. People from all around came to see him.

Fragment Two

While John was baptizing, many people from Jerusalem came to him, including the Pharisees, who were also baptized.

He wore a robe made from camel's hair and had a leather belt around his waist. His food was wild honey mixed with oil cakes, which tasted similar to manna.

Fragment Three

Many people came to be baptized, and Jesus was one of them. As he came up from the water, the sky opened, and he saw the Holy Spirit come down like a dove and enter him.

Then a voice from heaven said, "You are my chosen one, and I am pleased with you."

The voice continued, "Today, I have given you new life."

Suddenly, a bright light filled the place. John looked at Jesus and asked, "Who are you, Master?"

The voice from heaven spoke again, saying, "This is my chosen one, and I am pleased with him."

John fell to the ground at Jesus' feet and said, "Please, Master, baptize me."

But Jesus refused and said, "This must be done this way to complete what is meant to happen."

Fragment Four

A man named Jesus, who was about thirty years old, chose us to follow him.

He then went to Capernaum and entered Simon Peter's house.

He spoke and said, "While walking along the Sea of Tiberias, I called John and James, the sons of Zebedee, along with Simon, Andrew, Thaddaeus, Simon the Zealot, and Judas Iscariot. I also called you, Matthew. When you were sitting at your tax booth, I asked you to follow me, and you did."

"That is why you twelve will be my messengers, spreading my teachings across Judea."

Fragment Five

"Hey, your mother and brothers are outside waiting for you."

"Who is my mother? Who are my brothers?"

He pointed to his disciples and said, "These are my brothers, my mother, and my sisters—anyone who follows my Creator's will."

Fragment Six

"I am here to stop the practice of sacrifices."

"If you keep making sacrifices, your suffering will continue."

Fragment Seven

"Where do you want us to prepare your Passover meal?"

He said, "I don't want to eat this Passover lamb with you."

Epistle of the Apostles & Patristic Excerpts

Introduction

The Epistle of the Apostles (Latin: Epistula Apostolorum), despite its relatively obscure status today, is one of the most intriguing and illuminating documents in early Christian literature. Thought to have been composed during the second century CE, the text provides readers with a profound glimpse into how the early Christian community understood the resurrection of Christ, the nature of salvation, and the foundational apostolic teachings that underpinned their faith. As an apocryphal work, it offers a distinct perspective on theological controversies and doctrinal formation that shaped Christianity in its formative years.

The Epistle of the Apostles is not simply another apocryphal document—it holds a unique position due to its literary form. Presented as an epistle or letter, it is purportedly written by the apostles themselves, addressed to believers everywhere, serving as both encouragement and instruction. Unlike most epistles found in the New Testament canon, this text weaves narrative, prophecy, and theological discourse into a compelling literary tapestry. At its core, it claims to record a dialogue between the risen Christ and his apostles after the resurrection, adding layers of depth and meaning to its presentation.

Despite its omission from the canonical scriptures, this ancient text sheds invaluable light on early Christian beliefs, eschatological expectations, and the broader socio-cultural context of its original audience. As you embark on exploring the Epistle of the Apostles, this introduction aims to equip you with historical background, interpretive insights, and an understanding of its continuing relevance and appeal.

Historical and Cultural Background

The precise date and authorship of the Epistle of the Apostles remain subjects of scholarly debate. Nonetheless, most academics agree that it emerged between 120 and 180 CE, making it roughly contemporaneous with other significant early Christian texts such as the letters of Ignatius of Antioch and Justin Martyr's apologies. Its composition during this period places it squarely within the vibrant milieu of early Christianity, characterized by theological debate, doctrinal experimentation, and intense spiritual fervor.

The geographical origins of the epistle are uncertain, but scholars typically suggest either Asia Minor (modern-day Turkey), Syria, or Egypt as likely locations. This region was marked by diverse communities of believers who grappled with integrating Jewish traditions, Greco-Roman philosophical concepts, and emerging Christian theology. The epistle reflects these complexities, blending traditional apostolic teachings with the concerns and interests prevalent among second-century believers.

One significant characteristic of the Epistle of the Apostles is its intentional response to the growing influence of Gnostic teachings. Gnosticism—a diverse religious movement that proposed salvation through secret knowledge (gnosis)—had become influential in various regions, posing a considerable challenge to orthodox Christian beliefs. Gnostic teachers promoted esoteric revelations, often diminishing the physical resurrection of Jesus, portraying him instead as a purely spiritual being. The epistle directly confronts these assertions, strongly reaffirming both the bodily resurrection and the physical incarnation of Christ.

The second-century Christian communities, living under the shadow of persecution and doctrinal controversy, deeply valued writings that could strengthen their faith and clarify essential beliefs. The Epistle of the Apostles reflects the urgency and intensity of this period, offering believers reassurance in the authenticity and authority of apostolic tradition.

Content, Structure, and Themes

At first glance, the Epistle of the Apostles presents itself as an authoritative apostolic document—a letter from the very disciples who witnessed Christ's ministry, death, and resurrection. It opens by declaring itself a revelation received directly from Jesus by his closest followers. Throughout the epistle, the apostles relay Christ's teachings, their significance, and their implications for Christian life.

Structurally, the epistle combines elements of letter-writing with a gospel-like narrative. After introductory greetings and declarations of authenticity, the text recounts detailed dialogues between Jesus and the apostles. Jesus answers numerous questions posed by his followers regarding salvation, resurrection, judgment, the nature of God, and the role of faith and works in the believer's life. These conversations present a richly interactive portrayal of Christ as an engaged teacher, illuminating divine mysteries.

One key theme prominent throughout the text is the defense of orthodox belief in the physical reality of Christ's resurrection. In a direct response to Gnostic doctrines, the epistle emphasizes repeatedly the tangible nature of Jesus's risen body. This emphasis is intended to affirm the value and sanctity of the material world, countering Gnostic disparagement of physicality.

Another central theme is eschatological urgency. The Epistle of the Apostles vividly presents end-times scenarios, judgment, and the second coming of Christ. It underscores the immediate importance of repentance, ethical living, and the pursuit of righteousness. Early believers, living in expectation of Christ's imminent return, would have found profound encouragement in these passages. The detailed, often dramatic depictions of judgment and salvation reinforce the urgency and moral seriousness with which early Christians approached their faith.

Moreover, the epistle places great emphasis on the universal scope of salvation. Contrary to exclusivist Gnostic doctrines, it presents Christ's message as intended for all humanity, underscoring the apostolic mission to evangelize the world. This inclusive vision underscores the expansive, boundary-crossing nature of early Christianity, characterized by its willingness to engage diverse cultures and peoples.

Significance and Modern Relevance

In studying the Epistle of the Apostles, contemporary readers gain valuable insights into early Christian theology, spirituality, and communal identity. Though classified as apocryphal, its themes and concerns resonate powerfully with ongoing theological conversations within modern Christianity. Issues addressed within its pages—such as the tension between faith and works, the nature of bodily resurrection, and the balance between spiritual knowledge and orthodox belief—continue to engage believers and scholars alike.

For students of church history, this text offers an invaluable window into the debates and theological developments of the second century. It provides tangible evidence of early Christian responses to heretical movements, illustrating the active role texts played in shaping and defending doctrinal orthodoxy. Its direct engagement with Gnosticism allows modern readers to better understand why and how orthodox Christianity formed its core doctrines and why certain ideas were accepted or rejected.

Additionally, the epistle's literary qualities make it accessible and compelling. Its narrative form, imaginative dialogue, and vivid portrayals of Christ's teachings create an immersive reading experience. The text's imaginative richness serves both theological education and spiritual edification, inspiring readers toward deeper reflection on the mysteries of faith, the nature of salvation, and the lived experience of following Christ.

On a practical level, contemporary readers can appreciate how the epistle speaks to enduring human concerns about mortality, hope, and ethical conduct. Its messages of resurrection hope, divine judgment, and universal salvation continue to inspire and challenge. Reading this text encourages reflection on one's personal spiritual journey, the importance of faithful adherence to foundational beliefs, and the value of community in shaping and sustaining faith.

Approaching the Text

As you prepare to engage deeply with the Epistle of the Apostles, consider approaching it not only as a historical artifact but also as a living document, filled with insights and spiritual wisdom applicable today. Allow yourself to enter the world of early Christians, imagining their struggles, hopes, and aspirations. Reflect on how the apostles and early believers grappled with the foundational questions of faith—questions that still resonate deeply with modern seekers.

This introduction has provided historical, cultural, and thematic contexts to enrich your reading. As you journey through its pages, consider how the apostles' teachings might inform contemporary understandings of faith, community, and the nature of divine revelation. Observe how the text integrates narrative, theology, and practical spirituality into a cohesive whole, demonstrating how early Christians creatively communicated profound spiritual truths.

Ultimately, the Epistle of the Apostles invites you to a dialogue—a conversation across centuries. Engage its contents with curiosity, openness, and critical reflection. Allow it to provoke questions, inspire deeper thought, and perhaps even challenge existing beliefs. In doing so, you participate in a rich tradition of theological exploration and spiritual discovery that has characterized Christianity since its earliest days.

May your reading of the Epistle of the Apostles be both enlightening and transformative, deepening your understanding of early Christianity and enriching your own spiritual journey.

Epistle of the Apostles

Jesus Christ shared this message with his followers. He gave it to his apostles so they could pass it on to everyone. But there were people like Simon and Cerinthus who pretended to teach the truth, but really misled others with lies that bring harm. No one should follow them. This message was written to help you stay strong, stay calm, and stay true to the good news you've already heard. We remembered what was shared with us and wrote it down so the whole world could hear it too. We gladly bless you—our sons and daughters—in the name of God the Father, ruler of all, and of Jesus Christ. May you always receive more of God's grace.

We, the apostles—John, Thomas, Peter, Andrew, James, Philip, Bartholomew, Matthew, Nathanael, Judas the Zealot, and Cephas—are writing to churches everywhere, from every corner of the earth. We're sharing what we personally experienced with Jesus Christ. After he rose from the dead, we saw him, listened to him, and touched him. He showed us incredible things that were both powerful and true.

We know this for sure: Jesus Christ, our Lord and Savior, is God's Son. God, who created everything, sent him. Jesus is known by many names and is greater than all other powers. He is King of kings and Lord of lords. He sits in heaven, next to God the Father, above even the angels. Through his word, the sky was made. He formed the earth and all that lives on it. He gave the oceans their borders and made the rivers and springs flow. He created day and night, placed the sun and moon in the sky, and set the stars in place. He separated light from darkness. He created all the seasons—the rain, snow, hail, and cold—and gave each season its time. He causes earthquakes and settles the earth again. He made people in his image, to be like him. Long ago, the prophets spoke about him. The apostles preached about him. His followers touched him. We believe in Jesus, the Son of God. He became human and was born to Mary, a virgin, through the Holy Spirit—not because of human desire, but because it was God's plan. He was wrapped in cloth and laid in a manger in Bethlehem. He grew up, and we witnessed it all.

Once, Joseph and Mary sent Jesus to school. His teacher told him, "Say the letter A." Jesus replied, "Tell me what B means first." This story is true and well known.

Later, there was a wedding in Cana, a town in Galilee. Jesus was invited along with his mother and his brothers. At the wedding, he turned water into wine. He brought people back to life and helped those who couldn't walk. He healed a man with a paralyzed hand. A woman who had been bleeding for twelve years touched the edge of his robe and was healed right away. When we were amazed by what happened, Jesus asked, "Who touched me?" We said, "Lord, there are so many people around you." But he said, "I felt power go out from me." The woman stepped forward and said, "Lord, I touched you." Jesus replied, "Go. Your faith has made you well."

He helped deaf people hear and blind people see. He cast out evil spirits and healed those with skin diseases. One man who had many demons shouted, "Are you here to get rid of us before our time?" Jesus told them, "Leave this man and don't harm him." The demons went into a herd of pigs, which then ran into the water and drowned.

Jesus once walked on the sea during a storm. The wind was strong, but he told it to stop, and everything became calm. Another time, we didn't have money to pay taxes. We asked him what to do. He said, "Throw a hook into the water. The fish you catch will have a coin in its mouth. Use that to pay for both of us." On another day, we only had five loaves of bread and two fish. Jesus told the huge crowd—about five thousand men, not including women and children—to sit down. We handed out the food, and everyone ate until they were full. There were even twelve baskets of leftovers. We asked each other, "What do these five loaves mean?" They are a sign of our faith in God the Father, in Jesus Christ our Savior, in the Holy Spirit, in the church, and in the forgiveness of sins.

Jesus taught and showed us all these things. We're sharing them so you can receive God's grace too, join in our mission, and focus on eternal life. Stay strong in your belief in Jesus Christ. He will be kind to you and save you forever.

Simon and Cerinthus are still traveling around, but they are against Jesus Christ. They twist the truth and try to destroy faith in him. Stay far away from them. They are full of evil, and one day they will face judgment and be destroyed forever.

That's why we are writing to you about what Jesus, our Savior, did when we were with him. He helped us understand the truth clearly.

We declare that Jesus was crucified between two criminals, under the rule of Pontius Pilate and Archelaus. He was buried in a place called "The Skull." Three women—Mary (a relative of Martha), and Mary

Magdalene—went to his tomb carrying spices to care for his body. They were crying and grieving. But when they got there, they found that his body was gone. The stone had been rolled away and the entrance was open.

While they were crying, Jesus appeared and said, "Why are you crying? I'm the one you're looking for. Go tell the others that I have risen from the dead." Martha went and told us. We said, "Why are you telling us this? He's dead and buried. How could he be alive?" We didn't believe her. She told Jesus, "None of them believe you're alive." He said, "Send someone else to tell them." Mary went and told us again, but we still didn't believe. She also went back and told him.

Then Jesus said to the women, "Let's go to them." He found us and called us out, but we thought he was just a ghost and didn't believe it was really him. He said, "Come here. Don't be afraid. It's me. Peter, you denied me three times—are you going to do it again?" We came closer, but we still had doubts in our hearts. He said, "Why do you still doubt and not believe? I already told you about my death and rising again. But to help you know it's really me—Peter, touch the marks in my hands. Thomas, feel the wound in my side. Andrew, look at my feet and see if they leave footprints. The prophet wrote that spirits don't leave footprints on the ground."

We touched him so we could know for sure that he had truly risen in a real body. Then we fell to the ground, realizing our mistake in not believing sooner. Our Lord and Savior said to us, "Stand up, and I will show you what is beyond the heavens, what is in heaven, and the rest that waits for you in God's kingdom. My Father has given me the power to bring you there—and not only you, but everyone who believes in me."

Then he told us, "This is what I want you to know. Before I came here from the Father of all things, I passed through the heavens. As I traveled, I took on the wisdom and strength of the Father. When I entered heaven, I looked like one of the angels and passed through the ranks of archangels and heavenly powers. They thought I was one of them because I carried the wisdom of the one who sent me. The leading angel is Michael, and Gabriel, Uriel, and Raphael followed me up to the fifth level of heaven. They believed I was one of them because the Father gave me that power.

"That day, I amazed the archangels with a powerful voice, and they went to the altar of the Father to serve until I returned. I did this through my wisdom. I became everything to everyone, so that I could complete the Father's plan and bring honor to the one who sent me before going back to him."

"You know that Gabriel was the angel who brought the message to Mary," he said. We replied, "Yes, Lord." He said, "Don't you remember that I told you not long ago that I became an angel among the angels and took on many forms? On the day I appeared to Mary as Gabriel, I spoke with her. She welcomed me in her heart and believed. Then I shaped myself inside her and entered her body. I became human. I was the one who brought the message to her—I didn't send anyone else. I had to do it that way. After that, I returned to my Father."

He continued, "You must remember my death. When Passover comes, one of you will be arrested because of my name. That person will feel deep sorrow because you'll be celebrating Easter while he is locked away and can't be with you. But I will send my power through my angel Gabriel, and the prison doors will open. He will come to you and spend the night with you until the rooster crows. After you've remembered me through the meal of love, he will go back to prison again. This will be a sign for others, and afterward, he will be released and go preach what I taught you."

We asked him, "Lord, do we really need to keep drinking from the cup again? Didn't you already complete the Passover?" He answered, "Yes, you need to keep doing it until the day I return, along with those who died for me."

Then we said, "Lord, what you're revealing to us is incredible. But when you return, will it be in the form of a living creature or in some other way?" He replied, "Truly, I tell you, I will come like the rising sun, but even brighter—seven times brighter. The clouds will carry me in glory, the sign of the cross will come before me, and I will come to judge both the living and the dead."

We asked him, "Lord, when will all this happen?" He said, "When one hundred and one-twentieth of the time is fulfilled—between the feast of Pentecost and the feast of unleavened bread—then the coming of my Father will take place."

We asked, "But didn't you just say you would come? And now you're saying the one who sent you is the one who will come?" He replied, "I am fully in the Father, and the Father is fully in me." We asked, "Will you leave us until then? Who will be our teacher?" He said, "Don't you understand? Just as I've been here with you, I've also been there with the one who sent me." We said, "Lord, is it even possible for you to be in both places at once?" He answered, "Yes. I am completely in the Father, and he is in me. We are the same in form, in power, in completeness, in light, in truth, and in voice. I am the Word, the full expression of his thoughts, made real in human form. I have entered the highest place—the Lord's Day."

After Jesus was crucified, died, and rose again, and once everything was completed, including his return to heaven, he said this to us: "You will see the full purpose of everything after the redemption I brought. You will see me go to my Father in heaven. But now,

I give you a new command: Love one another. Obey one another, so peace will always be among you. Love even your enemies. And never do to anyone what you wouldn't want done to you."

"Teach this to everyone who believes in me. Share the message of my Father's kingdom. Tell them that the Father gave me the power so that you can help bring his children close to him. Preach with faith, so that those who are chosen can be brought to heaven."

We said, "Lord, you can surely do everything you've told us. But how can we do it?" He replied, "Truly, I tell you, go out and preach exactly as I've told you. I will be with you. I want to be with you, so you can share in the kingdom of heaven with me—the kingdom of the one who sent me. I promise you, you will be my brothers and friends. My Father is pleased with you. And all who believe because of your message will also be called my friends. I tell you, my Father has prepared so much joy for you that even the angels and heavenly beings have longed to see it. But they have not been allowed to see the full glory of my Father."

We said to him, "Lord, what exactly is this that you're telling us about?"

Copt. begins again: words are missing.

Jesus said, "You're going to see a light that's brighter than anything you've ever seen before. It will be more perfect than anything you can imagine. The

Son becomes perfect through the Father because the Father gives life, causes death, and brings the dead back to life. I am completely one with the Father, who makes everything complete."

We said, "Lord, everything you do gives us life and hope. You've given us so much to look forward to." He replied, "Be strong and rest in me. I promise you this—your rest will be in a place beyond this world. In that place, there's no hunger, no thirst, no sadness, no fear, and no death. You won't belong to the world anymore. You'll live forever with my Father. Just as I live in him, you'll live in me."

We asked, "What will we be like? Will we look like angels or like people?" He answered, "I became human, just like you. I was born in a body, I died in it, and I came back to life through my Father in heaven. This fulfilled what David the prophet said about me:

Lord, a lot of people are against me.

They say, "God won't save him."

But you, Lord, are my shield and you lift me up.

I cried out to you, and you answered me from your holy place.

I lay down to sleep, and I woke up because you kept me safe.

I won't be scared, even if thousands of enemies are all around me.

Get up, Lord! Save me, my God!

You hit my enemies and took away their power.

You, Lord, are the one who saves, and you bless your people.

"If the prophets' words about me came true—and I was with them when they spoke—then what I'm telling you now will also come true. My Father will be honored through you and everyone who believes in me."

We said, "Lord, you've shown us so much kindness, saved us, and told us everything we need. Can we ask one more thing?" He said, "I know you're truly seeking to understand. So go ahead and ask."

Then he said, "Just as my Father raised me from the dead, he will also raise you. You'll rise in your bodies and be taken to the highest heaven—the place I've always told you about. My Father has prepared it for you. I'll keep all my promises. Even though I wasn't born like everyone else, I became human so you could also rise again in bodies that never die. That's what my Father wants—to give this hope to you and to everyone I choose."

We said, "Lord, your words give us so much hope." He asked, "Do you really believe everything I say will happen?" We said, "Yes, Lord." He replied, "I have all my Father's power now. I will lead people out of darkness and into the light. I will raise the dead and set the trapped free. What people can't do, my Father can. I am hope for the hopeless, help for the helpless, treasure for the poor, healing for the sick, and life for the dead."

We asked, "Lord, will our bodies be judged along with our souls and spirits? Will one part go to heaven and the other be punished forever?" He said, "Why do you keep asking and doubting?"

We said, "Lord, we ask because you told us to teach others. We need to understand so we can help others believe." He said, "Yes, your body will rise again with your soul and spirit." We asked, "But how can something that's broken and gone come back to life? We believe you, Lord, we just want to understand." He looked disappointed and said, "Why do you still have so little faith? How long will you keep asking questions? But go ahead—ask, and I'll answer. Just keep my commandments. Do what I've taught you. Don't ignore others, so I won't turn away from you. Be brave. Be fair. Follow the straight path. Then my Father will be glad."

We said, "Lord, we feel bad for asking so many questions." He said, "I know your questions come from faith and a true heart. That makes me happy. My Father in me is happy too. Your desire to learn gives you life. It brings me joy." We were glad we had asked. We said, "Lord, you keep giving us life and showing us kindness. Can we ask one last question?" He said, "Tell me—what fades away: the body or the spirit?" We answered, "The body." He said, "Then what has fallen will rise again. What was lost will be found. What was weak will grow strong. And through all this, my Father's glory will be seen. What he did for me, I will do for everyone who believes in me."

He said, "Yes, the body will rise again with the soul. On the day of judgment, everyone will be judged for what they've done—good or bad. Those who obeyed my Father's commands will be chosen. The judgment will be fair. My Father said to me, 'My Son, when judgment day comes, don't favor the rich or feel sorry for the poor. Judge everyone by what they've done. The disobedient will be punished forever, but the obedient will live forever in my kingdom and see what I gave to you.' He gave me the power to fulfill his will and give the rewards I promised."

He continued, "That's why I went to the place where Lazarus was. I spoke to the prophets and the faithful who had died. I brought them out of their place of rest and raised them to something higher. I gave them life, forgiveness, and freedom from evil—just like I've done for you and for all who believe in me. But if someone believes in me and doesn't obey my commands—even if they say my name—it won't help them. Their belief is useless if they ignore what I say. They'll be lost."

He said, "That's why I've worked so hard to save you, the children of light, from evil and the power of this world's rulers. Everyone who believes in me because of your message will also be saved. I'll give them the same promises I gave you. They'll be free from the prison and chains of this world." We said, "Lord, you've given us eternal life and filled us with joy through your miracles. Will you teach us again like you taught the prophets and faithful people?" He said, "Truly, everyone who believes in me and the one who sent me will be taken to heaven—to the place my Father has prepared for the chosen. I will give you the kingdom, a place of rest and eternal life."

"But anyone who disobeys my commands, or teaches something different, twisting the Scriptures to gain attention, will be punished forever. If they lead faithful people the wrong way, they'll be judged for it." We asked, "Lord, will people really teach things that go against what you taught us?" He answered, "Yes, it will happen. That's how people will see the difference between good and evil. Those who do wrong will be judged by their actions."

We said, "Lord, we are so blessed to see you and hear your words. We've seen your miracles with our own eyes." He said, "Yes, you are blessed. But even more blessed are those who believe without seeing. They'll be called children of the kingdom. They will be counted among the perfect, and I will give them life in my Father's kingdom."

Then we said, "Lord, how will people believe when you're gone? You said one day you'll go back to your Father."

He answered, "Go and tell the twelve tribes of Israel, and also preach to people everywhere—from the east to the west, and from the south to the north. Many will believe in me, the Son of God." We asked, "Lord, who will believe us? How can we do the miracles you did?" He said, "Go and share the kindness of my Father. What he did through me, I will do through you. I live in you. I'll give you peace and the power of my Spirit. You'll speak the truth and lead people to eternal life. And I'll give that same power to others, so they can teach the rest of the world too."

(Six leaves lost in Copt.: Eth. continues.)

Jesus said, "You'll meet a man named Saul—his name also means Paul. He's a Jew who follows the law closely. He'll hear my voice from heaven and be so afraid that he shakes. He'll go blind, but through your hands and the sign of the cross, he'll be healed. Do for him what I've done for you. Share God's message with him. When that happens, his eyes will open, and he'll thank my Father in heaven. He'll be given power to speak among the people. He'll teach and preach, and many will listen, believe, and be saved. But later, people will become angry with him. They'll turn him over to his enemies. He'll speak boldly in front of kings. And though he used to fight against me, in the end, he'll return to me. He'll teach alongside the faithful. He'll be like a strong wall that can't be knocked down. Even though he started last, he'll become a preacher to non-Jews, chosen and made ready by my Father—just as the prophets said about me, and now it has all come true."

Then Jesus told us, "You also need to guide others. Everything I've taught you, and everything you write about me, teach others too. Help them understand that I am the Word from the Father, and the Father lives in me. Do the same for Paul—remind him of the Scriptures that speak about me. He will become a light for the people who don't yet know God."

We asked, "Lord, do we have the same hope of your promise as they do?" He said, "Are all fingers the same? Do all plants in a field look alike? Do all trees grow the same fruit? Of course not. Everything is different in its own way." We said, "Lord, are you using another example to teach us?" He answered, "Don't be upset. I'm telling you the truth—you are my brothers and my friends in the kingdom of heaven. My Father is happy with you. And the people you teach who believe in me will also share in this promise."

We asked again, "When will we meet Paul? And when will you go back to your Father, who is our God and Lord?" He said, "Paul will come from Cilicia and travel to Damascus in Syria. He wants to destroy the church you'll build there. But I'll speak through you, and he'll show up soon. He will become strong in faith. This will fulfill the prophecy that says: 'From Syria, I will begin building a new Jerusalem. Zion will belong to me. The one who had no children will be called my Father's child, my son and daughter, and my bride.' That's what the one who sent me wants. But I will stop Paul from doing evil. My Father's name will be honored through him. After I return home to be with my Father, I will speak to Paul from heaven. Everything I told you about him will happen."

We said, "Lord, you've told us so many amazing things—things we've never heard before. After you rose from the dead, you explained everything we needed to know to be saved. But you also said there would be strange signs in the sky and on earth before the world ends. Can you tell us how we'll recognize when that time is near?" He replied, "I'll explain—not just for you, but for those you will teach, and for anyone who believes in me, including those who listen to Paul. These things will happen in the future."

We asked, "What will happen?" He said, "Everyone—believers and nonbelievers—will hear a trumpet sound from heaven. Bright stars will be seen even during the day. Strange sights will appear in the sky, reaching down to earth. Stars will fall like fire. There will be a powerful firestorm. A bright star will rise from the east, glowing like fire. The sun and moon will appear to fight each other. There will be loud thunder, constant lightning, and earthquakes. Cities will collapse, and many people will die. There won't be rain, leading to long droughts. A terrible disease will spread, causing many deaths—so many that people won't be buried. Families will carry the bodies of their loved ones together. No one will help their neighbor. The dead will see the ones who harmed them. The sickness will bring pain, hatred, and jealousy. People will steal from each other. And it will get worse than ever before. How sad for those who didn't follow my commandments."

Jesus said, "Then my Father will be angry at the evil in the world. People will have sinned too much. Their dirty way of living will be too much to ignore."

We asked, "What about the people who trust you?" He replied, "You still don't fully understand. How much longer will it take? The prophet David spoke about me and my people. The same will happen to those who truly believe in me. But liars and enemies of truth will fulfill what David wrote: 'Their feet are quick to hurt others. Their words are full of lies. Poison hides behind their lips like snakes. They hang out with thieves and cheat on their partners. They talk badly about their own family and set traps for their brothers. Do they really think I'm just like them?' David said all this so that everything would happen just as he wrote."

We asked, "Lord, won't other nations say, 'Where is their God now?'" Jesus said, "That's how the chosen ones will be known—by how they come through tough times." We asked, "Will they die from painful disease?" He replied, "No. If they suffer, it will test whether they have faith, remember my words, and follow my commands. These people will rise again. Their suffering won't last long. That way, the one who sent me will be praised, and I will be praised with him. He sent me to tell you these things so you can share them with Israel and the non-Jews. Then they, too, can be saved, believe in me, and escape destruction. But if someone avoids death and still does wrong, they will be caught and punished like a thief."

We asked, "Lord, will believers be punished the same as nonbelievers? Will you punish those who escape disease?" He answered, "If someone says they believe in me but lives like a sinner, then it's like they never believed at all." We asked again, "Lord, do people who suffer have any hope?" He said, "Anyone who honors my Father will find rest with him."

We asked, "Lord, what comes after that?" He said, "In those days, wars will keep breaking out. All four corners of the earth will be in conflict with each other. Dark skies will cover the land. There will be food shortages and attacks on my followers. Many will say they believe in me, but they'll do evil and spread lies. People will follow them because they want wealth, pride, and pleasure. They'll care more about pleasing rich sinners than doing what's right."

"But those who truly want to see God and don't care about the wealth of sinful people—those who stand up for the truth even when it's hard—my Father will honor them. Those who speak up and correct their neighbors will also be saved. They are children of wisdom and faith. But if they don't live with wisdom, and if they hate and hurt their own brothers without helping them, then God will reject them."

(Copt. resumes.)

People who live honestly, trust in the faith, and love me—even when they're insulted—will be honored. They stayed loyal even when they were poor. Others hated and mocked them. They were treated badly for being hungry and thirsty. Still, they didn't give up. Because of their patience, they will be blessed in heaven and live with me forever. But those who are proud and always want attention will be lost in the end.

We asked, "Lord, is this really your plan? Are you going to leave us so these things can happen?" He said, "What kind of judgment would that be—fair or unfair?" We said, "Lord, won't people say you didn't treat right and wrong differently? That you didn't separate light from darkness or good from evil?" He answered, "I'll tell them this: God gave Adam the choice between two paths. He chose the light and held on to it, and he let go of the darkness. That means everyone now has the choice to believe in the light—which is life—and that light comes from the Father who sent me. Anyone who believes in the light and does what's right will live in the light. But if someone says they belong to the light but keeps doing dark things, they won't have anything to say in their defense. They won't even be able to look at the Son of God—that's me. I'll say to them, 'You got exactly what you were looking for. Why are you blaming me? Why did you walk away from me and deny me? Why did you say you believed but then turn against me?' Everyone has the power to choose life or death. Those who obey my commands are children of the light, children of the Father who lives in me. I came down from heaven because people were twisting what I said. I am the Word. I became human. I worked hard and taught that those who are burdened will be saved, but those who stray will stay lost forever. They will suffer in their bodies and souls."

We said, "Lord, we feel really sad for those people." He replied, "That's good. People who love what's right care about others and pray for them, asking my Father to help." We asked, "Is there anyone who can pray for them?" He said, "Yes, and I will listen to the prayers of those who are good and faithful."

Then we said, "Lord, you've taught us so much. You've been kind and saved us so we can help save others. Will we get a reward from you?" He answered, "Go and share the good news. You'll be workers, like parents and helpers." We said, "Lord, will you speak through us?" He said, "Aren't there many kinds of parents, teachers, and helpers?" We said, "But Lord, you told us not to call anyone on earth our father because we only have one Father in heaven. And now you're saying we'll be like fathers, teachers, and helpers?" He answered, "Yes, you got it right. I'm telling you the truth: anyone who hears you and believes in me will receive the light through me, and be baptized through me. So yes, you will be like fathers, teachers, and servants."

We asked, "Lord, how can we be all three at once?" He said, "You'll be called fathers because you shared the good news with love and helped others learn about the kingdom of heaven. You'll be called servants because through your hands people will be baptized and have their sins forgiven, with my power. You'll be called teachers because you shared the truth without holding anything back. You corrected people, and they listened. You weren't afraid of their money or status. You followed my Father's commands and stayed true. You will receive a great reward from my Father in heaven. And those you helped will be forgiven and live forever in the kingdom."

We said, "Lord, even if we had ten thousand tongues, we couldn't thank you enough for all the promises you've given us." He replied, "Just do what I told you, just like I've done myself."

"You'll be like the wise women who stayed awake and were ready to meet the groom. The foolish ones didn't stay awake, and they missed it." We asked, "Lord, who are the wise and who are the foolish?" He said, "There are five wise and five foolish. The prophet called them children of God. Listen to their names."

We started to cry and felt sorry for those who missed it. Jesus said, "The five wise are Faith, Love, Grace, Peace, and Hope. People who have these will lead others who believe in me and in the One who sent me. I am the Lord and the groom. They accepted me and joined me in my wedding celebration with joy."

"But the five foolish ones fell asleep. When they woke up, they came to the door and knocked, but it was closed. They cried and begged, but no one let them in."

We asked, "Lord, didn't the wise ones inside feel sorry for them? Didn't they ask you to open the door for them?" He said, "They couldn't help them." We asked, "Lord, will they ever be allowed in because of their sisters?" He answered, "Once someone is shut out, they really are shut out." We asked, "Lord, is that the final word?" He replied, "These are their names: Knowledge, Understanding, Obedience, Patience, and Compassion. These were in people who believed in me and said they followed me, but they didn't obey my commands."

"Because of that, they will stay outside the kingdom, away from the shepherd and the flock. Those who are outside will be attacked by wolves. They'll suffer badly. They won't find rest. Even though they're punished with long and painful torment, they won't find death quickly."

We said, "Lord, everything you said is clear." He asked, "Don't you understand these things?" We said, "Yes, Lord. Five will enter the kingdom, and five won't. The ones who stayed awake are with you, the groom, even though they feel sad for the others." He said, "They'll be happy to be with me, but they'll still feel sorrow because the others are their sisters. All ten are daughters of God, the Father." We said, "Lord, won't you help them because of their sisters?" He said, "That decision belongs to the One who sent me. I agree with whatever He decides."

"Be strong. Teach the truth. Don't be afraid of anyone, especially not the rich. They don't follow my commands and only brag about their money." We asked, "Lord, is it only the rich?" He said, "If a poor man gives even a little to someone in need, people call him generous."

"But if someone sins and feels guilty, and their neighbor helped them in the past, that neighbor should help them change. If the person listens and changes, they'll be saved, and the one who helped will be rewarded and live forever. But if someone sees their neighbor sinning and says nothing—even after that neighbor helped them before—they'll be judged harshly."

"If a blind person leads another blind person, they'll both fall into a hole. If you treat people unfairly just because of who they are, it's like being blind. The prophet said, 'Woe to those who treat people unfairly and protect wrongdoers just for money. Their stomach is their god.' That's the kind of judgment they'll face. I'm telling you the truth—on that day, I won't treat the rich any better or show pity to the poor."

"If you see someone doing wrong, talk to them privately. If they listen, you've helped them. If they don't, bring two or three others to talk with them. If they still won't listen, treat them like someone outside your group."

(Copt. defective from this point.)

If someone keeps ignoring correction, treat them like a stranger or an outsider.

If you hear something bad about your brother, don't believe it right away. Don't enjoy gossip or help spread it. It is written: Don't let your ears take in anything against your brother. But if you actually see something wrong, correct him, speak honestly, and try to help him change.

We said to him, "Lord, you've taught and warned us about everything. But what about those who already believe in you, those who are supposed to follow your message—will there still be arguments, jealousy, confusion, hate, and envy among them? You said they'll accuse one another, respect sinners, and dislike those who try to correct them."

He answered, "How else can there be judgment? The good grain has to be gathered into the storehouse, and the useless parts burned away."

He continued, "Those who hate evil, love me, and correct others who break my commandments will be hated, bullied, and made fun of. People will lie about them and team up to fight against those who love me. But the ones who speak up to help save others will be rejected and pushed aside. They'll be treated badly, even though they mean well. But anyone who can go through all this and stay faithful will be like the martyrs—they'll be with the Father, because they chose what's right instead of giving in to evil."

We asked him, "Lord, will this happen to us?" He replied, "Don't be afraid. It won't happen to many, just a few." We asked, "Then please tell us how it will happen." He said, "A new teaching will come that causes confusion. Because people will chase after their own goals, they'll start spreading a useless message. That message will be full of harmful ideas, and they'll teach it to others. It will lead believers away from my commandments and keep them from eternal life. But it will be terrible for those who twist my words and lead others away from the true path. They will face judgment forever, along with those who follow them."

After he said all this and finished talking with us, he told us again, "Look, on the third day at the third hour, the One who sent me will come, and I will go with Him."

While he was still speaking, there was thunder, lightning, and an earthquake. The sky opened, and a bright cloud appeared and lifted him up. Then we heard many angels singing joyfully and saying, "Bring us into the light of glory, O Priest." As they got close to the heavens, we heard his voice one last time saying to us, "Go in peace."

Thank You for Reading

Dear Reader,

We hope this timeless classic has sparked your imagination and enriched your literary journey. Now that you've turned the final page, we want to share a vision for the future of reading—one where every classic you've ever wanted to explore is at your fingertips, in a format that best suits your life.

We'd like to invite you to gain immediate, unlimited digital & audiobook access to hundreds of the most treasured literary classics ever written—along with the option to secure deluxe paperback, hardcover & box set editions at printing cost. Together, we can spark a new global literary renaissance alongside our small, independent publishing house called "The Library of Alexandria."

Thousands of years ago, the Library of Alexandria stood as a beacon of knowledge—until it was lost to history. We aim to reignite that spirit of preservation and discovery right now, in the modern age—only this time, it's accessible to all, in every language and every format.

Picture a world where every timeless classic, novel, poem, or philosophical treatise is not only available to read but also updated for today's readers—modernized, translated into any language or dialect, and ready to enjoy in any format you choose, whether that is in an eBook, audiobook, paperback, or deluxe hardcover & box set version a printing cost.

By joining our movement to rebuild the modern Library of Alexandria, you become part of an unprecedented mission to offer:

- **Unlimited Audiobook & eBook Access to the Greatest Classics of All Time**

    Instantly explore thousands of legendary works, from Plato and Shakespeare to Jane Austen and Leo Tolstoy. All are instantly ready to read or listen to, giving you a complete literary universe at your fingertips.

- **Paperback & Deluxe Editions at Printing Costs:**

    Purchase any title in a paperback, deluxe hardbound, or deluxe boxset edition at printing costs, shipped right to your doorstep. Curate your personal library of Alexandria with editions worthy of display—crafted to last, designed to captivate, and delivered straight to your door.

- **Modern translations for Contemporary Readers in all languages and dialects**

    Discover a vast selection of classics reimagined in clear, current language—no more struggling with outdated phrases or obscure references. Next to the original versions, we aim to offer translations in as many languages and dialects as possible.

As we continue our translation efforts and add new languages, readers everywhere can connect with these works as if they were written today. By bridging linguistic divides, you're contributing to ensuring that these timeless stories become more meaningful, accessible, and inspiring for people across the globe.

- **Your Personal Library of Alexandria:**

  Over the months and years, you'll curate a unique physical archive of classics—each volume a testament to your taste, curiosity, and love of knowledge. It's not just about owning books—it's about curating a cultural legacy you'll cherish and pass down for generations to come.

- **Join a Global Literary Renaissance:**

  Your support fuels an ongoing mission: allowing us to reinvest in offering deluxe print editions (including special boxsets) at their true cost, broaden the range of available formats and translations, and extend the reach of these works to new audiences worldwide. By joining today, you're not just preserving a legacy of masterpieces; you set in motion a powerful wave of literary accessibility.

We are more than a publisher—we're a movement, and we can't do it alone. Your support lets us scale our mission, preserving and reimagining history's greatest works for tomorrow's readers.

Become a Torchbearer of knowledge.

Thank you for picking up this book and allowing us into your literary journey. As you turn the pages, know that you're part of something larger: a global effort to keep these stories alive, share their wisdom across borders and generations, and spark a true cultural revival for the modern era.

If this resonates with you—please consider taking the next step by visiting:

www.libraryofalexandria.com

With gratitude and a shared love of knowledge,

The Modern Library of Alexandria Team

Visit:

www.libraryofalexandria.com

Or scan the code below:

www.ingramcontent.com/pod-product-compliance
Lightning Source LLC
LaVergne TN
LVHW030631080426
835512LV00021B/3457